True You Super You

Living true to YOU is Your superpower

AUDREY & AJ NESBITT

To AJ. You are and forever will
always be my superhero!
Mom

My wonderful girl.
AJ, you inspire me every day.
Dad

Super
You
Sparkle
Crew

AJ wakes up each morning feeling tired yet joyful. She is happy and free. She wiggles to push off the quilt and thinks really hard about picking out the right clothes; the clothes that make her feel special. The clothes that make her feel just right.

She pulls on her favourite purple glittery top, her beautiful purple skirt and her sparkly shoes. They help her stand a little taller and feel a lot stronger. Even though she is just 6 years old she knows better than anyone who she really is!

She says hello to her mum, who smiles with pride at how confidently her daughter walks through the house. It reminds her that she too should live her life being more true to herself.

AJ eats her breakfast and prepares her things for school.
She fills her bag with her favorite notebook and pens,
the ones with purple fluff and pink tassels.

Walking to school alone, AJ continues to stand tall with her shoulders back. Even when people turn and look, she shrugs, she has the power of being more true to herself.

At school, her friends greet AJ, all smiling broadly. Tommy, who used to be Tammy, is in his school trousers and a hockey jersey. He is proud to be himself too, even though mean kids shout that he should still be wearing a skirt cause he's really a girl. He never liked being a girl just like AJ never felt right as a boy.

Ruby and Jake, Ellie and Ashley huddle in and make the group known as the Super You Sparkle Crew.

This is a school like any other school. Most kids are nice, but there are bullies in some of the corridors. The teachers are wonderful, they work hard to keep all students safe. But people will be people and people can be mean.

In the schoolyard, AJ's girl friends are talking about boy crushes and she joins in. Other kids overhear and AJ hears the same nasty comments all the time.

Kids shout that AJ will never be a real girl and that she will always be a boy. She pulls her purple cardigan tight and stands up straight.

She reaches school and faces another daily challenge. The washrooms are labelled with a boy and a girl. AJ knows the kids will stare but she knows where to go.

But the voices all around her shout and make her feel strange for choosing the girls' room. She has the power to be true to herself and this allows her to break through the noise. So what? She thinks. She knows who she is.

Tommy lingers in front of the washrooms. He never knows what to do. He wants to use the boy's room, but it is scary in there. Jake comes along at just the right time and Tommy follows him into the bathroom. Jake is Tommy's best friend and as part of the Super You Sparkle Crew, knows about sharing one's superpower.

AJ's teacher, Miss Stapleton, watches as the students file back into class. Miss Stapleton is proud of all of her students, but especially AJ. She sometimes wishes that she, too, could live her life being more true to herself.

Sitting on a seat in the far corner is Paul. He is shy with small round glasses and hair that spikes in all directions. He is a new student and is very clever, but he pretends to not understand the work or know the answers. The other kids in the class can be mean to people who show off what they know.

AJ makes it clear to the Super You Sparkle Crew that she plans to sit next to Paul and help him feel more accepted. AJ likes to transfer some of her superpowers to others who deserve to live their lives being more true to themselves.

AJ takes the seat next to Paul and works alongside him through math. AJ asks for his help and he is so grateful he blushes. AJ makes it clear she wishes she were as clever as Paul.

Paul is still quite shy, even when AJ transfers some of her superpowers. But he would like to be more true to himself and will try to be braver each day. He puts his hand up and shows the class he is clever.

Lunchtime comes and it's time for food. AJ says hello to Cook Thomas, who smiles at AJ and wishes he had some of her superpowers so he could live being more true to himself too. He really wants bright purple hair and a mohawk but keeps it short, neat and ordinary.

Ruby, Ellie and Ashley join AJ at their bench in the schoolyard. They chat and giggle. Martin kicks a ball at AJ's back. It is not by accident and everyone knows this. AJ smiles and says, "Never mind. I am sure Martin feels sorry for what he has done." She pulls her purple cardigan tight and stands up straight.

Martin laughs and jeers. He does feel a little sorry for kicking the ball, but he wants to be popular. He also wants to be a kind person. He is not sure how to be who he wants to be. He just knows he gets attention when he's disruptive. He doesn't hate AJ. He secretly likes her and hopes one day to be her friend. Being more true to one's self can be more difficult for others.

The day continues, and it is time for gym class. AJ hates gym class. She is not comfortable changing in front of other girls in the changeroom. She uses a washroom away from her friends and heads to the field in her shorts and t-shirt.

Tommy has a hard time too. But AJ and Tommy both have superpowers that are strong enough to see them through.

Next is Geography and AJ is as happy as ever. Tommy is a bit sad and sits alone. He was teased by the other boys in gym class.

AJ can understand how he feels and often feels this way herself. She sits beside him and works quietly. Tommy is grateful. He likes her company and feels better because she is there with him. They are both in this together and that gives them more superpowers.

AJ, Tommy, Jake, Ruby, Ashley and Ellie finally get to be the Super You Sparkle Crew as the last school bell rings for the end of the day. They laugh and giggle. They chat about the day and share their stories.

The school day is over, and all is well. AJ can go home and put on her favorite dress. She runs through the front door and up the stairs. Her dress is pink, white, and blue, just like some of her other favorite superheroes.

Her mum asks about her day and AJ tells her everything. Being honest about the ups and downs is part of being a good superhero. AJ's mum gives her a big bear hug and tells her she is proud she is her daughter. AJ has looked forward to this hug all day because it gives her all of her superpowers.